Taking

by Ricardo Ramos
illustrated by Julia Gorton

HOUGHTON MIFFLIN   BOSTON

ISBN 10: 0-618-88613-3
ISBN 13: 978-0-618-88613-5

789 0940 16 15 14 13 12
4500365496

Everywhere I go, I look for shapes.
I like to find shapes in shapes.
Today, I'm going to the city.
What shapes will I find?
I think I will take pictures!

The first thing I see is a billboard.

This shape is a rectangle.

I also see other shapes in it.

Do you see them, too?

Read • Think • Write What shapes do you see within the
rectangle? How many do you count?

At our next stop, I see different shapes.

I see a rectangle in the middle.

I see two parts of another shape on the ends.

Do you see them, too?

Read • Think • Write   What other shape do the two parts make?

I walk across a sky bridge.

It has many shapes.

Inside those shapes, I see other shapes.

Do you see them, too?

Read • Think • Write What shapes are on the sides
of the bridge? What shapes are within those?

I look up at a tall building.

It looks like a cake!

Near the top, I see shapes.

Do you see them, too?

Read • Think • Write What shapes are near the top?

Before going home, I stop at an old building.
It has windows with 8 sides.
In the windows, I see other shapes.
Do you see them, too?

Read • Think • Write What do you call an
eight-sided shape?

7

Shapes Inside Shapes

Show

Look at page 3. Draw the billboard and the shapes in the billboard.

Share

Summarize Look at page 3. Tell about the shapes of the billboard.

Write

Look at page 3. Write the name of the shapes in the billboard.